The Constitution of the United States of America

———◆———

With the Declaration of Independence and the Articles of Confederation

Introduction by R. B. Bernstein

FALL RIVER PRESS

Introduction © 2002 by Fall River Press

Fall River Press
122 Fifth Avenue
New York, NY 10011

ISBN: 978-0-7607-2833-8

Printed and bound in the United States of America

17   19   21   23   25   24   22   20   18

Table of Contents

Introduction

The sacred rights of mankind are not to be rummaged for among old parchments or musty records. They are written, as with a sunbeam, in the whole volume of human nature, by the hand of the divinity itself, and can never be erased.

Alexander Hamilton,
The Farmer Refuted (1775).

These documents, written on "old parchments" squirreled away among "musty records," remain living realities *because* they eloquently record the sacred rights and responsibilities of human beings. We still think about the enduring challenges of government in terms coined by the Revolutionary generation of Americans. They thought more deeply and argued more vigorously about these challenges than any generation after them, leaving us a series of unprecedented experiments in nation-building and constitution-making. We often forget just how revolutionary the creation of the United States was. However, the Americans of that era never forgot it. Revisiting these documents enables us to grasp the American experiment's revolutionary quality.

I. The Declaration of Independence
The Declaration of Independence, the central document of American political life, codifies the American political creed. To understand it, however, we must know its origins and purpose. The Declaration was the last American word in the argument between Great Britain and its

American colonists. In 1763, the British Empire, the most successful and the freest the world had seen, had no more loyal subjects than the colonists of the thirteen mainland colonies of British North America. Within two years, however, the first stirrings of disagreement between Britain and the colonists began to disturb peace within the Empire. Two years after the end of the French and Indian (Seven Years') War, Britain confronted massive war debts. Convinced that the colonists had had a free ride on the backs of British taxpayers, British politicians decided to redress the balance by taxing them, but the colonists protested these taxes as unconstitutional.

This controversy put the nature of the British constitution into dispute. Unlike the United States Constitution, the British constitution is not one authoritative document framed and adopted at a specific time. Rather, it is the mass of laws, judicial decisions, documents having constitutional status (such as the Magna Carta), and customs making up, or *constituting*, the British government. Because the British constitution is unwritten, an array of understandings of its principles could spring up. Two of these marked out the opposing positions between the colonists and Britain.

The colonists saw the British constitution as a restraint on arbitrary power. Each of its three major institutions—the Crown, the House of Lords, and the House of Commons— had the power to check the other two. Arbitrary (unchecked) power went beyond actual tyranny to include potential tyranny. When Parliament made laws for the colonies as the empire's supreme authority, it was acting arbitrarily. In particular, taxation without representation was tyranny. Parliament could not tax the colonists, because they could not vote for members of the House of Commons. Only the colonial legislatures could tax the colonists.

By contrast, the British happily gave Parliament its role as the supreme institution in their constitutional system. Parliament had earned this role by defending liberty against the Stuart kings Charles I and James II. Each member of the House of Commons represented not just those who elected him, but all the King's subjects. Under this idea of *virtual* representation, Parliament could tax the colonists and make laws for them, though they were not actually represented.

In arguing with Britain, the thirteen colonies, which previously were closer to the mother country than to one another, learned that they had a common cause—defending their liberties. This insight, fostered by the Stamp Act Congress of 1765 and the First Continental Congress of 1774, led them to see themselves as Americans.

By 1776, the argument between Britain and the colonies had reached a stalemate. The British were not listening to the Americans, and had sent British soldiers to bring the colonists under control. The reality of war (which began at Lexington and Concord in 1775) opened American minds to the idea of independence from Britain. That January, Thomas Paine's pamphlet, *Common Sense*, offered a powerful case for independence. Beginning by demolishing monarchy (the last linchpin of American loyalty to Britain), Paine showed that the Americans deserved independence and could win it, persuading hundreds of thousands to see independence as legitimate and desirable.

Four months later, in May 1776, the Second Continental Congress directed the colonies to frame new constitutions to replace their colonial charters. Americans' commitment to liberty, the core principle of Anglo-American constitutionalism, was pushing them out of the Empire. That June, Richard Henry Lee of Virginia introduced three resolutions in the Second Continental Congress, the first declaring that the colonies "are, and of right ought to be, free and independent states." On July 2, 1776, Congress adopted those resolutions; two days later, it adopted a declaration drafted by Thomas Jefferson, setting forth the Americans' case against George III and for independence.

The Declaration looks in two directions at once. It looks backward, as the last American word in the argument with Britain, and forward, charting the future political development of an independent America. It indicted George III because the king had spurned his last chance to avoid a breach with the colonies. Its famed preamble was key to its case against the king. Its citing of "inalienable rights" and "life, liberty, and the pursuit of happiness" formed the basis on which Americans could invoke the right of revolution against the tyrant George III. And yet, the Declaration's preamble also states the principles on which Americans would build their constitutions and political systems and govern themselves. Americans have continued to invoke the Declaration to advance the cause of democracy, equal rights, and individual liberty, at home and around the world. Thus, the document by which the Second Continental Congress justified declaring independence found a life of its own as a cultural, political, and constitutional symbol, eclipsing the act it was intended to explain.

II. The Articles of Confederation

Just as it took time for Americans to break with Britain, it took time for them to see themselves as (in Hamilton's words in *The Federalist No. 85*) "a nation without a national government" and take steps to remedy that defect. In the process, they had to prepare the political ground for governmental reform, and to devise mechanisms and institutions that they wanted to assemble as a new national constitution.

Beginning in 1776, Americans launched a series of experiments in state constitution-making. The fruits of those experiments guided later efforts in devising and amending constitutions (including, in 1787, framing the U.S. Constitution). But, in 1776, few Americans felt that they needed a national government. For one thing, they recalled the failure of the British empire; for another, they were devoted to a body of principles called *republicanism*.

Americans wanted republican government, which meant no king and no nobility. The people, the ultimate source of legitimate power, would exercise it through their elected representatives. But conventional wisdom taught that a republic could work only with a small population in a small territory. Each of the thirteen states was as big as a republic could be to survive external and internal threats to its existence. Thus, it seemed unlikely that one government over all thirteen states could survive and preserve liberty.

In July 1776, when Congress adopted Lee's resolution for independence, they also adopted his two other resolutions. The first authorized negotiations with such European powers as France and Spain; the second called for "articles of confederation and perpetual union." On November 15, 1777, after a year of argument, Congress sent the Articles of Confederation to the states. The Articles created a one-house Confederation Congress, with each state having one vote. Most issues required a majority, and such matters as treaties needed a two-thirds vote. All thirteen states had to ratify any proposed amendment. The Confederation had no independent executive or judiciary, no power to raise revenue, and no power to operate directly on individuals.

How would the Confederation be financed? Because the Confederation Congress had no taxing power, it had to ask the states for money (with each state's share based on the value of its lands). The states were to collect taxes and send the proceeds to the Confederation. Americans distrusted a strong central government, especially one with taxing power. They were fighting a revolution against one such government and were leery of trusting another. Also, Congress, caught up in the Revolution's fervor, believed that faith in the cause would spur the states to do what they were asked to do.

It took nearly four years for all thirteen states to ratify the Articles. Under the Articles, the United States established relations with the Netherlands, France, Morocco, Prussia, and Spain; borrowed money abroad to help finance the war; and fielded a Continental Army that won the war. Its diplomats won the peace, negotiating the Treaty of Paris (1783) under which Britain recognized American independence and gave the United

States all territory between the Allegheny Mountains and the Mississippi River.

The Confederation's greatest domestic achievement had to do with those western lands. Some states claimed these lands, based on colonial charters, but their claims overlapped. Other states, which had no land claims, resented that "landed" states had a chance to make windfall profits by selling land to settlers and investors. The "landless" states refused to ratify the Articles of Confederation until the landed states transferred their claims to the United States, so that the nation could reap this windfall. The next problem was governing these lands. Under "territorial ordinances" that Congress adopted in 1784, 1785, and 1787, these lands were organized as territories, to be admitted to the Union as new states on an equal basis with the original thirteen, with rules for organizing local government and for public education. Slavery would not be allowed north of the Ohio River (the Northwest Territory). Thus, Congress abandoned the old model of colonialism—a mother country governing territories as colonies only in its own interests.

Despite these successes, the Articles had fundamental weaknesses that threatened the Union. Also, state economic and political problems (which the Confederation could not resolve) threatened the American experiments in government. .

The Treaty of Paris pledged Americans to honor debts owed to British or Loyalist creditors—but the states ignored these promises; angered, Britain refused to withdraw from the western territories. Also, Britain, France, and Spain limited trade with the new nation—

which could not retaliate or force the lifting of these limits. Third, Spain controlled the lower Mississippi, strangling American settlements—unless American settlers swore allegiance to Spain. Again, the United States was powerless to resist.

The Confederation had repeated difficulties with the states. They rarely paid what they owed the Confederation in full or on time; some never paid at all. They also ignored treaties with Indian nations. Many states failed to send delegates to Congress—often leaving Congress unable to function. The Confederation could not force states to meet their obligations, and it could not amend the Articles to give Congress more power. States disputed boundaries, argued over fishing rights, waged trade wars against one another, and imposed tariffs on goods imported across state lines—all to bolster their own economies at their neighbors' expense. Also, settlers in frontier regions of New York, Virginia, Massachusetts, and North Carolina tried to found independent states—and Congress could not help resolve these disputes.

Most alarming, turmoil between debtors and creditors convulsed many states, a problem worsened by the economic downturn of the mid-1780s. Hardest hit were farmers, who lived from harvest to harvest and could be ruined by one bad year. In Rhode Island, battles between debtor and creditor parties led to rapidly-changing state laws, such as paper-money laws, that helped debtors but hobbled interstate commerce and seemed to nervous creditors to attack the rights of private property.

Where debtors could not win relief through politics, they rebelled against what they saw as heartless creditors and an indifferent judicial system. The most famous debtors' rebellion was Shays's Rebellion, which began in western Massachusetts. Outbreaks of debtor violence spread beyond that state, from Vermont to Virginia; by some estimates, one-fourth of the armed men of New England took part in Shays's Rebellion. Daniel Shays, a former captain in the Continental Army, was more a symbol of revolt than an actual leader of the rebellion; he was a debt-ridden farmer who struggled to keep a roof over his family's head. In January of 1787, Massachusetts authorities (with the help of the Continental Army) put down Shays's Rebellion, but its lessons lingered.

III. The Making of the Constitution

In the mid-1780s, Americans who thought in national terms argued that the problems plaguing the Confederation required a revolution in government. They revived the political process that between 1765 and 1776 had created the revolutionary movement. In 1785, at the Mount Vernon Conference, delegates from Virginia and Maryland settled boundary disputes and navigation rights. Virginia then proposed a convention to meet at Annapolis, Maryland, in September 1786 to solve national commercial problems. Only delegates from Virginia, New York, Delaware, Pennsylvania, and New Jersey showed up at Annapolis, but they seized the chance to redefine the American political agenda. They proposed a new convention to meet in Philadelphia in 1787, "to render the constitution of government adequate to the exigencies of the Union." On February 21, 1787, the Confederation Congress endorsed this proposal, but its more limited resolution, stressing revision of the Articles, clashed with the Annapolis mandate.

Of the 74 delegates from 12 states (Rhode Island refused), only 55 showed up at the Convention at some point. Some of the greatest American politicians were not there. John Adams was American Minister to Great Britain. Thomas Jefferson was American Minister to France. John Jay was the Confederation's Secretary for Foreign Affairs in New York City. Patrick Henry stayed in Virginia because he was uninterested in national politics, although he later claimed, "I smelt a rat."

Five kinds of delegates attended the Convention. *National heroes* George Washington of Virginia and Benjamin Franklin of Pennsylvania brought prestige, guaranteeing that Americans would give the Convention's proposals a fair hearing. *Theorists of government*, such as James Madison of Virginia, James Wilson of Pennsylvania, and Alexander Hamilton of New York, brought ideas that the Convention would use to frame its proposals. *Elder statesmen*, such as John Dickinson of Delaware and Roger Sherman of Connecticut, brought their experience (one of two reality checks on the Convention). *Advocates of local interests*, such as William Paterson of New Jersey and Luther Martin of Maryland, spoke for the states' concerns (the other reality check). Finally, most delegates—such *quiet men* as John Blair of Virginia and Jacob Broome of Delaware—became raw material for consensus and compromise.

From May 25 through May 28, the delegates elected their president, George Washington, and their secretary, William Jackson of Georgia, and adopted rules. From

May 29, when Edmund Randolph of Virginia proposed the resolutions known as the Virginia Plan, to June 14, the large-state delegates prevailed on nearly every issue. The Virginia Plan outlined a national government with supreme legislative, executive, and judicial branches. On June 15, the small-state delegates counterattacked, backing William Paterson's New Jersey Plan, which was nothing more than a reworking of the Articles of Confederation giving Congress more power. On June 19, the Convention reaffirmed the Virginia Plan—but large-state delegates and small-state delegates battled for weeks over representation in Congress. Small-state delegates fought for equality of states in Congress; large-state delegates demanded representation based on population. This conflict lasted through July 16, when the Convention adopted the Great or Connecticut Compromise. From July 19 to July 26, the delegates pored over the plan, tinkering and adjusting, and then recessed for a week. During the recess, Randolph prepared the Constitution's first draft, drawing on Wilson's advice.

The delegates reconvened on August 6. For the next five weeks, they tackled problems they had postponed, such as devising a method for choosing the President and Vice President. They also adopted compromises to appease the slave states. From September 10 to September 12, the Committee on Style and Arrangement drew up the Constitution's final draft (assigning this task to Gouverneur Morris of Pennsylvania). From September 12 to September 17, the delegates moved through the last stage of revision. On September 17, 1787, 37 of the 40 delegates present voted to adopt and sign the

Constitution, and to send it to the Confederation Congress.

No group at the Convention got its way—especially not the theorists of government. Senior statesmen warned them that they were going too far and too fast; localist politicians demanded fairness for state interests; and architects of compromise set their ideas aside. Nothing is more fatal to theoretical purity than the spirit of compromise. The Convention made a vitally important shift—from devising the best Constitution possible in theory to devising the best that had a chance to be adopted.

What kind of document did this process produce? The Constitution creates a government of three branches, with limited but generous grants of power to operate directly on individual citizens. The House of Representatives represents the people, and each state has equal representation in the Senate. The President is elected indirectly by an electoral college mixing national and federal elements; his powers, largely undefined, strike a balance between the good example of George Washington and the bad example of George III. The Constitution leaves the federal judiciary's structure to Congress. Although it includes compromise clauses dealing with slavery, the words "slavery" and "slave" appear nowhere in the document—because the framers hoped that future generations would find a solution to slavery or that slavery would die out. The amending process, codified in Article V, is easier to work than was Article 13 of the Articles of Confederation. And Article VI's Supremacy Clause makes the Constitution the supreme law of the land, and empowers federal courts to interpret it as part of their duties. Finally, because of fatigue and the belief, as Roger Sherman said, that it would be "unnecessary," the original Constitution lacked a bill of rights. That turned out to be a fateful decision.

Article VII set forth the process for adopting the Constitution. Each state would elect a ratifying convention. If nine of the thirteen state conventions (two-thirds) ratified it, it would go into effect as the new government of the United States. Two-thirds was easier to achieve than the unanimous consent required by Article 13. Also, the ratifying conventions were more likely than the state legislatures to consider the Constitution on its merits; the legislatures, jealous of their power, would resist any attempt to shift power to the general government. Finally, because the Constitution would be the government of the American people, only they, not the states, had the power to form such a government.

On September 26–28, 1787, the Confederation Congress debated the Constitution. Its opponents failed to persuade Congress to rewrite it or to reject it as exceeding the Convention's power, and its supporters failed to get Congress to endorse it. Instead, Congress silently forwarded the Constitution to the states (thus implying that the Constitution was legitimate).

The ratification controversy was the supreme display of American political creativity. It operated on two interacting levels. On the formal level, the Confederation Congress sent the Constitution to the state legislatures, which called elections for ratifying conventions, which deliberated on ratifying the Constitution. On the informal level, a vigorous argument over the Constitution raged through the nation—in newspapers, pamphlets, broadsides, and rallies. The informal argument may have been the more important level, for it launched American constitutional discourse—the ongoing shared argument among the people about the Constitution's origins, significance, meaning, and applications—and helped to create a national political community, focusing the people's attention on the political element of their national identity.

Who supported the Constitution (under the name Federalists)? Who opposed it (known to posterity as Anti-Federalists)? Some scholars argue that rich people tended to support the Constitution and poor or working-class people tended to oppose it, or that city-dwellers supported the Constitution and farmers opposed it. Both these distinctions fail. Modern scholars suggest that the national issue of ratification interacted in each state with pre-existing divisions of state politics, to produce a crazy-quilt of shifting alliances and loyalties. They focus on tracing links between Anti-Federalist and Federalist understandings of politics and society and their positions on the Constitution.

Anti-Federalists insisted that the Convention exceeded its mandate by writing a new Constitution instead of revising the Articles. Federalists retorted that Congress and the states had accepted the Constitution's legitimacy; thus, the issue was moot. Also, in *The Federalist No. 40*, Madison invoked the right of revolution in the Declaration of Independence. He pointed out that a government too weak to safeguard the Revolution was as threatening to liberty as a government that might be too strong.

Second, the two sides disagreed on the nature of the Union and the relationship between the Union and the states. Anti-Federalists feared that the general government would swallow up the states, destroying the people's right of self-government. Federalists, citing the history of the Confederation, insisted that the states would infringe on the general government's powers, as they had with the Confederation. Also, they urged that only a government at least as strong as that outlined in the Constitution could protect the general good and the people's liberties. Otherwise, the Union would break into separate confederacies—which, some Federalists charged, was what Anti-Federalists had in mind. Denying that they wanted to break up the Union, Anti-Federalists insisted that, even if the Confederation was too weak to safeguard American interests, the Constitution still was too dangerous.

Third, Anti-Federalists denounced the Constitution's system of representation as inadequate. They mocked the House of Representatives and the Senate as too small by comparison with the large state legislatures. They argued that this unjust scheme of representation would limit service in Congress to powerful, wealthy men. Federalists retorted that the Constitution's scheme of representation was designed to choose men of enlarged views, who could grasp the nation's interests; moreover, reapportionment would expand the House beyond its original size. Finally, Congress's powers were limited to avoid infringing the people's rights and the states' legitimate powers, yet extensive enough to safeguard the general good.

Anti-Federalists, distrusting the Presidency, charged that the President was not accountable, that impeachment was too difficult to use against him, and that he would work to ensure his repeated re-election ior life. Federalists retorted that the President would be accountable because he could not hide behind advisers; that his brief term of office would not make him a king; and that the electoral college would choose the best man for the job.

Anti-Federalists denounced federal courts as unnecessary and expensive. They worried that federal courts would swallow up state courts, wiping out distinctions between state laws and leaving the people subject to a tyrannous federal bench. They also decried the lack of trial by jury in civil cases. In response, Federalists justified the federal judiciary as a bulwark of liberty that would defend the Constitution against unconstitutional acts of the national legislature or executive and vindicate the Constitution and the general government against encroachments by the states.

Anti-Federalists found the Constitution's lack of a bill of rights their most powerful argument. Even many who backed the Constitution objected to its lack of a bill of rights. Jefferson scolded Madison: "A bill of rights is what the people are entitled to against every government on earth, and what no just government should refuse, or rest on inference." Federalists argued that a bill of rights was not needed, because the Constitution gave the federal government no power over rights. They also noted, as Hamilton insisted in *The Federalist No. 84*, that the Constitution itself was a bill of rights. But, aware that they were vulnerable on this issue, they began to rethink their position.

Federalists praised the Constitution's amending process (Article V). It would be easier to use than Article 13 of the Articles of Confederation, but it also would bolster the Constitution as a fundamental law that should not be lightly altered. Article V's blend of national and federal elements, as Madison noted in *The Federalist No. 39*, proved that the Constitution would neither destroy the states nor be at their mercy.

Other issues came up as well. Anti-Federalists objected to the clause authorizing a permanent capital, which would become a citadel where the people's enemies would shelter themselves against the people's wrath. Federalists highlighted the humiliating journeys of the Continental and Confederation Congresses from city to city during and after the Revolution; a new nation required the stability of a permanent capital. New England Anti-Federalists denounced the Constitution's ban on religious tests for voting or holding office, fretting that a Jew, a Turk, or an infidel could become President. Federalists extolled this ban as a bulwark of religious liberty. Anti-Federalists in New England also denounced the Constitution's slavery clauses (but Southern Federalists praised them).

The Constitution's amending process played a vital role in its victory. At the outset, some Anti-Federalists insisted that the Constitution had to be amended before they would accept it, drafting lists of "previous amendments." Other Anti-Federalists were willing to adopt the Constitution, but only with added "conditional amendments." By contrast, Federalists insisted that the Constitution had to be adopted or rejected without amendments. In February 1788, the Massachusetts ratifying convention found a sensible compromise. Anti-Federalists would prepare a list of "recommended amendments" to be sent to the first Congress to meet under the Constitution, and Federalists pledged to back such amendments. This device of recommended amendments became the key to the Constitution's victory; all states after Massachusetts (except Maryland) added lists of recommended amendments to their resolutions of ratification. These lists were the raw material from which Madison drew his list of proposed amendments that he offered in the House of Representatives of the First Congress on June 8, 1789. Ten of those amendments were ratified in 1791, becoming the Bill of Rights.

IV. Constitutional Change

Americans have shaped their lives through law, and for more than two hundred years the Constitution has been the core of the nation's law. We make many demands on the Constitution: it sets forth our government's structure, allocates powers and duties among our public institutions and officials, and defines our rights and responsibilities. Just as important, the Constitution declares the nation's central principles—the goals for which we came together as a nation; the purposes of its grants of power and limits on power; and the kinds of public and private lives that we want to foster under its protection.

The Constitution changes over time, in three major ways. The most sweeping is "formal constitutional change"—using Article V's amending process to add provisions to the Constitution. Formal constitutional change alters the document's form, by a method of lawmaking more formal and difficult to use than ordinary lawmaking. To become part of the Constitution, a proposed amendment must win a two-thirds vote in both houses of Congress, and then be ratified by three-fourths of the states (38 out of 50). More than 12,000 amendments have been proposed since 1789, but Congress has proposed only 33 to the states, and only 27 have been adopted.

Constitutional amendments fall into one of three categories. The first group (such as the first ten, the Bill of Rights) protects fundamental principles of liberty and self-government; some (the Civil War Amendments [XIII, XIV, XV]) extend protections of liberty in ways either not imagined by the Constitution's framers and ratifiers or developing their efforts. The second group (such as that providing that Senators be elected by each state's voters [XVII] or the voting-rights amendments [XV, XIX, XXIII, XXIV, and XXVI]) expands democracy as a core component of the constitutional system. And the third group (such as those dealing with the electoral college, Presidential terms of office, and Presidential succession and disability [XII, XXII, XXV]) repairs defects of the original Constitution or responds to problems not envisioned by the Constitution's framers and ratifiers.

The second way of changing the Constitution is judicial interpretation. Courts must apply the Constitution's provisions to changing times and circumstances; that is why Edmund Randolph, who prepared the first draft of the Constitution in August of 1787, wrote that he had to draft the Constitution in general terms. Such powerful phrases as "commerce among the several states," "freedom of speech," "cruel and unusual punishment," and "equal protection of the laws" change meaning over time, as new problems arise and people devise new responses to old problems. Each branch of the federal government, and state and local officials, must interpret the Constitution—but our system gives special weight to the interpretations set forth by federal courts, especially the United States Supreme Court.

Some of the pivotal moments of American history have come when the Supreme Court has had to interpret the Constitution to deal with a divisive issue, or to resolve a controversy between the other branches of government. For example, in 1857, Chief Justice Roger B. Taney seized the opportunity to interpret the Constitution authoritatively to resolve issues concerning slavery. In *Dred Scott v. Sandford*, Taney ruled that the federal government had no power to limit slavery's spread into the territories. The public outcry over this decision helped to bring on the Civil War four years later. In 1954, in *Brown v. Board of Education*, Chief Justice Earl Warren declared for a unanimous Supreme Court that racial segregation violated the Fourteenth Amendment's Equal Protection Clause. Just as *Dred Scott* has long been considered the low point of judicial interpretation of the Constitution, *Brown* has long been considered a high point. And, in 1974, in *United States v. Nixon*, Chief Justice Warren E. Burger ruled for a unanimous Supreme Court that President Richard Nixon had to obey a federal court's order to turn over tape recordings of private meetings with key aides as evidence in the Watergate investigations. This decision, upholding the principle of the rule of law against a sweeping claim of presidential authority, helped to force Nixon to resign his office.

Third, customs and usages grow up around the Constitution, helping to guide its day-to-day workings. Political parties are not mentioned in the Constitution, but they have become essential to the workings of the elected branches of government and to the conduct of elections. So, too, federal courts recognize "executive privilege" (the principle that a President's confidential discussions with his aides should stay confidential in most circumstances)—but not, as in *United States v. Nixon*, when records of those discussions may be essential to investigate alleged crimes.

These three forms of constitutional change work together in a complex series of interactions, but they all help to maintain the American constitutional system's ability to respond to new circumstances and conditions.

R. B. Bernstein
Adjunct Professor of Law
New York Law School
2002

Chronology

September 5 – October 26, 1774
First Continental Congress meets at Carpenters' Hall, in Philadelphia, to coordinate American resistance to British colonial policy.

April 19, 1775
Battles of Lexington and Concord, in Massachusetts, mark beginning of American War of Independence.

May 15, 1776
Second Continental Congress instructs states to adopt new constitutions of government.

July 2–4, 1776
Second Continental Congress declares American independence and adopts Declaration of Independence.

September 3, 1783
Signing of Treaty of Paris, under which Britain recognized American independence and ceded territory between Allegheny Mountains and Mississippi River to United States.

May 25, 1787
Federal Convention convenes in Philadelphia, in Assembly Room of Pennsylvania State House (Independence Hall).

July 13, 1787
Confederation Congress, meeting in New York City, adopts Northwest Ordinance.

September 17, 1787
Federal Convention adopts final text of proposed Constitution and dissolves.

June 21, 1788
New Hampshire's ratifying convention adopts proposed Constitution (89–79), becoming the needed ninth state putting the Constitution into effect as the form of government of the United States.

April 30, 1789
George Washington inaugurated as the first President of the United States, at Federal Hall in New York City.

December 15, 1791
Virginia ratifies ten proposed constitutional amendments, adding the Bill of Rights to the U.S. Constitution.

March 4, 1801
Thomas Jefferson inaugurated as third President of the United States in Washington, D.C., marking the first presidential inauguration in the nation's permanent capital.

February 24, 1803

Chief Justice John Marshall hands down the unanimous decision of the U.S. Supreme Court in *Marbury v. Madison*, establishing the doctrine of judicial review of federal statutes.

March 16, 1810

Chief Justice John Marshall hands down the decision of the U.S. Supreme Court in *Fletcher v. Peck*, establishing the doctrine of judicial review of state legislation under the Supremacy Clause of the Constitution.

March 6, 1857

Chief Justice Roger B. Taney hands down his opinion for the Court in *Dred Scott v. Sandford*, declaring that the federal government has no power to restrict the spread of slavery within the United States or its territories.

April 12, 1861

Beginning of Civil War, with surrender of Fort Sumter (in Charleston, South Carolina) to forces of Confederate States of America.

January 1, 1863

President Abraham Lincoln issues Final Emancipation Proclamation, declaring all slaves in states rebelling against the Union "forever free."

November 19, 1863
President Abraham Lincoln delivers Gettysburg
Address.

December 6, 1865
Ratification of Thirteenth Amendment (proposed
January 18, 1865), outlawing slavery in the United
States.

July 9, 1868
Ratification of Fourteenth Amendment (proposed
June 13, 1866), establishing equal protection of the
laws, supremacy of federal citizenship, and requiring
states to follow due process of law.

February 3, 1870
Ratification of Fifteenth Amendment (proposed
February 26, 1869), forbidding discrimination in access
to the polls on the basis of race, color, or previous condition of servitude.

May 18, 1896
U.S. Supreme Court decides *Plessy v. Ferguson*,
upholding "separate but equal" principle and thus
allowing state laws requiring segregation of the races.

August 18, 1920
Ratification of Nineteenth Amendment (proposed
June 4, 1919), forbidding discrimination in access to
the polls on the basis of sex.

April 12, 1937
U.S. Supreme Court decides *National Labor Relations Board v. Jones & Laughlin Steel Corporation*, upholding federal power to regulate labor relations.

May 17, 1954
U.S. Supreme Court decides *Brown v. Board of Education*, striking down school segregation as violation of Fourteenth Amendment's "equal protection" clause.

March 9, 1964
U.S. Supreme Court decides *New York Times Co. v. Sullivan*, imposing federal constitutional standards on libel suits brought by government officials against the news media.

July 2, 1964
Enactment of U.S. Civil Rights Act of 1964, upholding sweeping federal authority to enforce civil rights against state and local governments and to bar private discrimination.

June 7, 1965
U.S. Supreme Court decides *Griswold v. Connecticut*, recognizing constitutional protection for right of privacy in decisions about giving birth and using contraception.

June 13, 1966

U.S. Supreme Court decides *Miranda v. Arizona*, enforcing federal constitutional protection of rights of criminal suspects and defendants against state and local governments, origin of "Miranda warnings."

June 30, 1971

U.S. Supreme Court decides *New York Times v. United States* ("Pentagon Papers" case), rejecting idea that federal government can invoke national security as justification to prevent publication of news stories.

January 22, 1973

U.S. Supreme Court decides *Roe v. Wade*, upholding federal constitutional protection for a woman's right to decide whether or not to have an abortion.

July 24, 1974

U.S. Supreme Court decides *United States v. Nixon*, rejecting sweeping presidential claims of executive privilege and holding that a President must submit to a federal grand jury's demand for evidence in an ongoing investigation.

June 26, 1978

U.S. Supreme Court decides *Regents of the University of California v. Bakke*, recognizing the constitutionality of "affirmative action" programs.

June 29, 1992

U.S. Supreme Court decides *Planned Parenthood v. Casey*, upholding constitutional protection of women's right of choice.

December 12, 2000

U.S. Supreme Court decides *Bush v. Gore*, resolving disputed 2000 presidential election. Justices rule, 7–2, that proposed recount in Florida of disputed votes does not meet standards of "equal protection of the laws" set forth in Fourteenth Amendment and further rule, 5–4, that exigencies of deciding a presidential election rule out a further statewide recount.

The Constitution of the United States of America

THE CONSTITUTION OF THE UNITED STATES OF AMERICA

WE THE PEOPLE of the United States, in Order to form a more perfect Union, establish Justice, insure domestic Tranquility, provide for the common defence, promote the general Welfare, and secure the Blessings of Liberty to ourselves and our Posterity, do ordain and establish this Constitution for the United States of America.

Article I

Section 1.
All legislative Powers herein granted shall be vested in a Congress of the United States, which shall consist of a Senate and House of Representatives.

Section 2.
The House of Representatives shall be composed of Members chosen every second Year by the People of the several States, and the Electors in each State shall have the Qualifications requisite for Electors of the most numerous Branch of the State Legislature.

No Person shall be a Representative who shall not have attained to the Age of twenty five Years, and been seven Years a Citizen of the United States, and who shall not, when elected, be an Inhabitant of that State in which he shall be chosen.

[Representatives and direct Taxes shall be apportioned among the several States which may be included within this Union, according to their respective Numbers, which shall be determined by adding to the whole Number of free Persons, including those bound to Service for a Term of Years, and excluding Indians not taxed, three fifths of all other Persons.]* The actual Enumeration shall be made within three Years after the first Meeting of the Congress of the United States, and within every subsequent Term of ten Years, in such Manner as they shall by Law direct. The number of Representatives shall not exceed one for every thirty Thousand, but each State shall have at Least one Representative; and until such enumeration shall be made, the State of New Hampshire shall be entitled to chuse three, Massachusetts eight, Rhode Island and Providence Plantations one, Connecticut five, New York six, New Jersey four, Pennsylvania eight, Delaware one, Maryland six, Virginia ten, North Carolina five, South Carolina five, and Georgia three.

When vacancies happen in the Representation from any State, the Executive Authority thereof shall issue Writs of Election to fill such Vacancies.

The House of Representatives shall chuse their Speaker and other Officers; and shall have the sole Power of Impeachment.

---

* Changed by Section 2 of the Fourteenth Amendment.

Section 3.

The Senate of the United States shall be composed of two Senators from each State, [chosen by the Legislature thereof,]* for six Years; and each Senator shall have one Vote.

Immediately after they shall be assembled in Consequence of the first Election, they shall be divided as equally as may be into three Classes. The Seats of the Senators of the first Class shall be vacated at the Expiration of the second Year, of the second Class at the Expiration of the fourth Year, and of the third Class at the Expiration of the sixth Year, so that one third may be chosen every second Year; [and if Vacancies happen by Resignation, or otherwise, during the Recess of the Legislature of any State, the Executive thereof may make temporary Appointments until the next Meeting of the Legislature, which shall then fill such Vacancies.]*

No Person shall be a Senator who shall not have attained to the Age of thirty Years, and been nine Years a Citizen of the United States, and who shall not, when elected, be an Inhabitant of that State for which he shall be chosen.

The Vice President of the United States shall be President of the Senate, but shall have no Vote, unless they be equally divided.

---

* Changed by the Seventeenth Amendment.

The Senate shall chuse their other Officers, and also a President pro tempore, in the Absence of the Vice President, or when he shall exercise the Office of President of the United States.

The Senate shall have the sole Power to try all Impeachments. When sitting for that Purpose, they shall be on Oath or Affirmation. When the President of the United States is tried, the Chief Justice shall preside: And no Person shall be convicted without the Concurrence of two thirds of the Members present.

Judgment in Cases of Impeachment shall not extend further than to removal from Office, and disqualification to hold and enjoy any Office of honor, Trust, or Profit under the United States: but the Party convicted shall nevertheless be liable and subject to Indictment, Trial, Judgment, and Punishment according to Law.

Section 4.
The Times, Places and Manner of holding Elections for Senators and Representatives shall be prescribed in each State by the Legislature thereof; but the Congress may at any time by Law make or alter such Regulations, except as to the Places of chusing Senators.

The Congress shall assemble at least once in every Year, and such Meeting shall be [on the first Monday in December,]* unless they shall by Law appoint a different Day.

---

* Changed by Section 2 of the Twentieth Amendment.

Section 5.

Each House shall be the Judge of the Elections, Returns, and Qualifications of its own Members, and a Majority of each shall constitute a Quorum to do Business; but a smaller Number may adjourn from day to day, and may be authorized to compel the Attendance of absent Members, in such Manner, and under such Penalties as each House may provide.

Each House may determine the Rules of its Proceedings, punish its Members for disorderly Behavior, and, with the Concurrence of two thirds, expel a Member.

Each House shall keep a Journal of its Proceedings, and from time to time publish the same, excepting such Parts as may in their Judgement require Secrecy; and the Yeas and Nays of the Members of either House on any question shall, at the Desire of one fifth of those Present, be entered on the Journal.

Neither House, during the Session of Congress, shall, without the Consent of the other, adjourn for more than three days, nor to any other Place than that in which the two Houses shall be sitting.

Section 6.

The Senators and Representatives shall receive a Compensation for their Services, to be ascertained by Law, and paid out of the Treasury of the United States. They shall in all Cases, except Treason, Felony and

Breach of the Peace, be privileged from Arrest during their Attendance at the Session of their respective Houses, and in going to and returning from the same; and for any Speech or Debate in either House, they shall not be questioned in any other Place.

No Senator or Representative shall, during the Time for which he was elected, be appointed to any civil Office under the Authority of the United States, which shall have been created, or the Emoluments whereof shall have been increased during such time and no Person holding any Office under the United States, shall be a Member of either House during his Continuance in Office.

Section 7.
All Bills for raising Revenue shall originate in the House of Representatives; but the Senate may propose or concur with Amendments as on other Bills.

Every Bill which shall have passed the House of Representatives and the Senate, shall, before it become a Law, be presented to the President of the United States; If he approve he shall sign it, but if not he shall return it, with his Objections to that House in which it shall have originated, who shall enter the Objections at large on their Journal, and proceed to reconsider it. If after such Reconsideration two thirds of that House shall agree to pass the Bill, it shall be sent, together with the Objections, to the other House, by which it shall likewise be reconsidered, and if approved by two thirds of that House, it shall become a Law. But in all such

Cases the Votes of both Houses shall be determined by Yeas and Nays, and the Names of the Persons voting for and against the Bill shall be entered on the Journal of each House respectively. If any Bill shall not be returned by the President within ten Days (Sundays excepted) after it shall have been presented to him, the Same shall be a Law, in like Manner as if he had signed it, unless the Congress by their Adjournment prevent its Return in which Case it shall not be a Law.

Every Order, Resolution, or Vote, to which the Concurrence of the Senate and House of Representatives may be necessary (except on a question of Adjournment) shall be presented to the President of the United States; and before the Same shall take Effect, shall be approved by him, or being disapproved by him, shall be repassed by two thirds of the Senate and House of Representatives, according to the Rules and Limitations prescribed in the Case of a Bill.

Section 8.

The Congress shall have Power To lay and collect Taxes, Duties, Imposts and Excises, to pay the Debts and provide for the common Defence and general Welfare of the United States; but all Duties, Imposts and Excises shall be uniform throughout the United States;

To borrow money on the credit of the United States;

To regulate Commerce with foreign Nations, and among the several States, and with the Indian Tribes;

To establish an uniform Rule of Naturalization, and uniform Laws on the subject of Bankruptcies throughout the United States;

To coin Money, regulate the Value thereof, and of foreign Coin, and fix the Standard of Weights and Measures;

To provide for the Punishment of counterfeiting the Securities and current Coin of the United States;

To Establish Post Offices and Post Roads;

To promote the Progress of Science and useful Arts, by securing for limited Times to Authors and Inventors the exclusive Right to their respective Writings and Discoveries;

To constitute Tribunals inferior to the supreme Court;

To define and punish Piracies and Felonies committed on the high Seas, and Offenses against the Law of Nations;

To declare War, grant Letters of Marque and Reprisal, and make Rules concerning Captures on Land and Water;

To raise and support Armies, but no Appropriation of Money to that Use shall be for a longer Term than two Years;

To provide and maintain a Navy;

To make Rules for the Government and Regulation of the land and naval Forces;

To provide for calling forth the Militia to execute the Laws of the Union, suppress Insurrections and repel Invasions;

To provide for organizing, arming, and disciplining, the Militia, and for governing such Part of them as may be employed in the Service of the United States, reserving to the States respectively, the Appointment of the Officers, and the Authority of training the Militia according to the discipline prescribed by Congress.

To exercise exclusive Legislation in all Cases whatsoever, over such District (not exceeding ten Miles square) as may, by Cession of particular States, and the Acceptance of Congress, become the Seat of the Government of the United States, and to exercise like Authority over all Places purchased by the Consent of the Legislature of the State in which the Same shall be, for the Erection of Forts, Magazines, Arsenals, dock-Yards, and other needful Buildings;—And

To make all Laws which shall be necessary and proper for carrying into Execution the foregoing Powers, and all other Powers vested by this Constitution in the Government of the United States, or in any Department or Officer thereof.

Section 9.

The Migration or Importation of Such Persons as any of the States now existing shall think proper to admit, shall not be prohibited by the Congress prior to the Year on thousand eight hundred and eight, but a Tax or duty may be imposed on such Importation, not exceeding ten dollars for each Person.

The privilege of the Writ of Habeas Corpus shall not be suspended, unless when in Cases of Rebellion or Invasion the public Safety may require it.

No Bill of Attainder or ex post facto Law shall be passed.

No Capitation, or other direct, Tax shall be laid, unless in Proportion to the Census or Enumeration herein before directed to be taken.*

No Tax or Duty shall be laid on Articles exported from any State.

No Preference shall be given by any Regulation of Commerce or Revenue to the Ports of one State over those of another: nor shall Vessels bound to, or from, one State be obliged to enter, clear, or pay Duties in another.

---

* See Sixteenth Amendment.

No money shall be drawn from the Treasury, but in Consequence of Appropriations made by Law; and a regular Statement and Account of the Receipts and Expenditures of all public Money shall be published from time to time.

No Title of Nobility shall be granted by the United States: And no Person holding any Office of Profit or Trust under them, shall, without the Consent of the Congress, accept of any present, Emolument, Office, or Title, of any kind whatever, from any King, Prince, or foreign State.

Section 10.
No State shall enter into any Treaty, Alliance, or Confederation; grant Letters of Marque and Reprisal; coin Money; emit Bills of Credit; make any Thing but gold and silver Coin a Tender in Payment of Debts; pass any Bill of Attainder, ex post facto Law, or Law impairing the Obligation of Contracts, or grant any Title of Nobility.

No State shall, without the Consent of the Congress, lay any Imposts or Duties on Imports or Exports, except what may be absolutely necessary for executing its inspection Laws: and the net Produce of all Duties and Imposts, laid by any State on Imports or Exports, shall be for the Use of the Treasury of the United States; and all such Laws shall be subject to the Revision and Control of the Congress.

No State shall, without the Consent of Congress, lay any Duty of Tonnage, keep Troops, or Ships of War in time of Peace, enter into any Agreement or Compact with another State, or with a foreign Power, or engage in War, unless actually invaded, or in such imminent Danger as will not admit of delay.

Article II

Section 1.

The executive Power shall be vested in a President of the United States of America. He shall hold his Office during the Term of four Years, and, together with the Vice President, chosen for the same term, be elected, as follows:

Each State shall appoint, in such Manner as the Legislature thereof may direct, a Number of Electors, equal to the whole Number of Senators and Representatives to which the State may be entitled in the Congress; but no Senator or Representative, or Person holding an Office of Trust or Profit under the United States, shall be appointed an Elector.

[The Electors shall meet in their respective States, and vote by Ballot for two Persons, of whom one at least shall not be an Inhabitant of the same State with themselves. And they shall make a List of all the Persons voted for, and of the Number of Votes for each; which List they shall sign and certify, and transmit sealed to the Seat of the Government of the United States, directed to the President of the Senate. The President of the Senate shall, in the Presence of the Senate and House of Representatives, open all the Certificates, and the Votes shall then be counted. The Person having the greatest Number of Votes shall be the President, if such Number be a Majority of the whole Number of Electors appointed; and if there be more than one who have such Majority, and have an equal Number of Votes, then the House of Representatives shall immediately chuse by Ballot one of them for President; and if no Person have a Majority, then from the five highest on the List the said House shall in like Manner chuse the President. But in chusing the President, the Votes shall be taken by States the Representation from each State having one Vote; A quorum for this Purpose shall consist of a Member or Members from two thirds of the States, and a Majority of all the States shall be necessary to a Choice. In every Case, after the Choice of the President, the Person having the greatest Number of Votes of the Electors shall be the Vice President. But if there should remain two or more who have equal Votes the Senate shall chuse from them by Ballot the Vice President.]*

The Congress may determine the Time of chusing the Electors, and the Day on which they shall give their Votes; which Day shall be the same throughout the United States.

---

* Changed by the Twelfth Amendment.

No person except a natural born Citizen, or a Citizen of the United States, at the time of the Adoption of this Constitution, shall be eligible to the Office of President; neither shall any Person be eligible to that Office who shall not have attained to the Age of thirty five Years, and been fourteen Years a Resident within the United States. [In case of the removal of the President from Office, or of his Death, Resignation or Inability to discharge the Powers and Duties of the said Office, the Same shall devolve on the Vice President, and the Congress may by Law provide for the Case of Removal, Death, Resignation or Inability, both of the President and Vice President, declaring what Officer shall then act as President, and such Officer shall act accordingly, until the Disability be removed, or a President shall be elected.]*

The President shall, at stated Times, receive for his Services, a Compensation, which shall neither be increased nor diminished during the Period for which he shall have been elected, and he shall not receive within that Period any other Emolument from the United States, or any of them.

Before he enter on the Execution of his Office, he shall take the following Oath or Affirmation:—"I do solemnly swear (or affirm) that I will faithfully execute the Office of President of the United States, and will to the best of my Ability, preserve, protect and defend the Constitution of the United States."

---

* Changed by the Twenty-fifth Amendment.

Section 2.

The President shall be Commander in Chief of the Army and Navy of the United States, and of the Militia of the several States, when called into the actual Service of the United States; he may require the Opinion, in writing, of the principal Officer in each of the executive Departments, upon any Subject relating to the Duties of their respective Offices, and he shall have Power to grant Reprieves and Pardons for Offenses against the United States, except in Cases of Impeachment.

He shall have Power, by and with the Advice and Consent of the Senate to make Treaties, provided two thirds of the Senators present concur; and he shall nominate, and by and with the Advice and Consent of the Senate, shall appoint Ambassadors, other public Ministers and Consuls, Judges of the supreme Court, and all other Officers of the United States, whose Appointments are not herein otherwise provided for, and which shall be established by Law: but the Congress may by Law vest the Appointment of such inferior Officers, as they think proper, in the President alone, in the Courts of Law, or in the Heads of Departments.

The President shall have Power to fill up all Vacancies that may happen during the Recess of the Senate, by granting Commissions which shall expire at the End of their next Session.

Section 3.

He shall from time to time give to the Congress Information of the State of the Union, and recommend to their Consideration such Measures as he shall judge necessary and expedient; he may on extraordinary Occasions, convene both Houses, or either of them, and in Case of Disagreement between them, with Respect to the Time of Adjournment, he may adjourn them to such Time as he shall think proper; he shall receive Ambassadors and other Public Ministers; he shall take Care that the Laws be faithfully executed, and shall Commission all the Officers of the United States.

Section 4.

The President, Vice President and all civil Officers of the United States, shall be removed from Office on Impeachment for, and Conviction of, Treason, Bribery, or other high Crimes and Misdemeanors.

Article III

Section 1.

The judicial Power of the United States, shall be vested in one supreme Court, and in such inferior Courts as the Congress may from time to time ordain and establish. The Judges, both of the supreme and inferior Courts, shall hold their Offices during good Behaviour, and shall, at stated Times, receive for their Services a Compensation, which shall not be diminished during their Continuance in Office.

Section 2.

The judicial Power shall extend to all Cases, in Law and Equity, arising under this Constitution, the Laws of the United States, and Treaties made, or which shall be made, under their Authority;—to all Cases affecting Ambassadors, other public Ministers and Consuls;—to all Cases of admiralty and maritime jurisdiction;—to Controversies to which the United State shall be a Party;—to Controversies between two or more States;—[between a State and Citizens of another State;—]* between Citizens of different States,—between Citizens of the same State claiming Lands under the Grants of different States [and between a State, or the Citizens thereof;—and foreign States, Citizens or Subjects.]*

In all Cases affecting Ambassadors, other public Ministers and Consuls, and those in which a State shall be a Party, the supreme Court shall have original Jurisdiction. In all the other Cases before mentioned, the supreme Court shall have appellate Jurisdiction, both as Law and Fact, with such Exceptions, and under such Regulations as the Congress shall make.

The trial of all Crimes, except in Cases of Impeachment, shall be by Jury; and such Trial shall be held in the State where the said Crimes shall have been committed; but when not committed within any State, the Trial shall be at such Place or Places as the Congress may by Law have directed.

---

* Changed by the Eleventh Amendment.

Section 3.

Treason against the United States, shall consist only in levying War against them, or, in adhering to their Enemies, giving them Aid and Comfort. No Person shall be convicted of Treason unless on the Testimony of two Witnesses to the same overt Act, or on Confession in open Court.

The Congress shall have Power to declare the Punishment of Treason, but no Attainder of Treason shall work Corruption of Blood, or Forfeiture except during the Life of the Person attainted.

Article IV

Section 1.

Full Faith and Credit shall be given in each State to the public Acts, Records, and judicial Proceedings of every other State. And the Congress may by general Laws prescribe the Manner in which such Acts, Records and Proceedings shall be proved and the Effect thereof.

Section 2.

The Citizens of each State be entitled to all Privileges and Immunities of Citizens in the several States.

A Person charged in any State with Treason, Felony, or other Crime, who shall flee from Justice and be found in another State, shall on demand of the executive Authority of the State from which he fled, be delivered up, to be removed to the State having Jurisdiction of the Crime.

[No Person held to Service or Labour in one State, under the Laws thereof, escaping into another, shall, in Consequence of any Law or Regulation therein, be discharged from such Service or Labour, but shall be delivered up on Claim of the Party to whom such Service or Labour may be due.]*

Section 3.
New States may be admitted by the Congress into this Union; but no new State shall be formed or erected within the Jurisdiction of any other State; nor any State be formed by the Junction of two or more States, or Parts of States, without the Consent of the Legislatures of the States concerned as well as of the Congress.

The Congress shall have Power to dispose of and make all needful Rules and Regulations respecting the Territory or other Property belonging to the United States; and nothing in this Constitution shall be so construed as to Prejudice any Claims of the United States, or of any particular State.

Section 4.
The United States shall guarantee to every State in this Union a Republican Form of government, and shall protect each of them against Invasion; and on Application of the Legislature, or of the Executive (when the Legislature cannot be convened) against domestic Violence.

---

* Changed by the Thirteenth Amendment.

Article V

The Congress, whenever two thirds of both Houses shall deem it necessary, shall propose Amendments to this Constitution, or, on the Application of the Legislatures of two thirds of the several States, shall call a Convention for proposing Amendments, which, in either Case, shall be valid to all Intents and Purposes, as Part of this Constitution, when ratified by the Legislatures of three fourths of the several states, or by Conventions in three fourths thereof, as the one or the other Mode of Ratification may be proposed by the Congress; Provided that no Amendment which may be made prior to the Year One thousand eight hundred and eight shall in any Manner affect the first and fourth Clauses in the Ninth Section of the first Article; and that no State, without its Consent, shall be deprived of its equal Suffrage in the Senate.

Article VI

All Debts contracted and Engagements entered into, before the Adoption of this Constitution, shall be as valid against the United States under this Constitution, as under the Confederation.

This Constitution, and the Laws of the United States which shall be made in Pursuance thereof; and all Treaties made, or which shall be made, under the Authority of the United States, shall be the supreme Law of the Land; and the Judges in every State shall be bound thereby, any Thing in the Constitution or Laws of any State to the contrary notwithstanding.

The Senators and Representatives before mentioned, and the Members of the several State Legislatures, and all executive and judicial Officers, both of the United States and of the several States, shall be bound by Oath or Affirmation, to support this Constitution; but no religious Test shall ever be required as a Qualification to any Office or public Trust under the United States.

Article VII

The Ratification of the Conventions of nine States shall be sufficient for the Establishment of this Constitution between the States so ratifying the Same.

Done in Convention by the Unanimous Consent of the States present the Seventeenth Day of September in the Year of our Lord one thousand seven hundred and Eighty seven and of the Independence of the United States of America the Twelfth In witness whereof We have hereunto subscribed our Names,

Go. WASHINGTON — Presidt.
and deputy from Virginia

New Hampshire: JOHN LANGDON
                NICHOLAS GILMAN

Massachusetts:	NATHANIEL GORHAM
	RUFUS KING
Connecticut:	WM. SAML. JOHNSON
	ROGER SHERMAN
New York:	ALEXANDER HAMILTON
New Jersey:	WIL: LIVINGSTON
	DAVID BREARLEY
	WM. PATERSON
	JONA: DAYTON
Pennsylvania:	B FRANKLIN
	THOMAS MIFFLIN
	ROBT MORRIS
	GEO. CLYMER
	THOS. FITZ SIMONS
	JARED INGERSOLL
	JAMES WILSON
	GOUV MORRIS
Delaware:	GEO: READ
	GUNNING BEDFORD jun
	JOHN DICKINSON
	RICHARD BASSETT
	JACO: BROOM

Maryland:	JAMES MCHENRY
	DAN OF ST. THOS. JENIFER
	DANL CARROLL
Virginia:	JOHN BLAIR
	JAMES MADISON jr
North Carolina:	WM. BLOUNT
	RICHD. DOBBS SPAIGHT
	HU WILLIAMSON
South Carolina:	J. RUTLEDGE
	CHARLES COTESWORTH
	PINCKNEY
	CHARLES PINCKNEY
	PIERCE BUTLER
Georgia:	WILLIAM FEW
	ABR BALDWIN

ATTEST WILLIAM JACKSON SECRETARY

In Convention Monday, September 17th, 1787.

Present The States of
New Hampshire, Massachusetts, Connecticut, Mr. Hamilton from New York, New Jersey, Pennsylvania, Delaware, Maryland, Virginia, North Carolina, South Carolina and Georgia.

Resolved,
That the preceeding Constitution be laid before the United States in Congress assembled, and that it is the Opinion of this Convention, that it should afterwards be submitted to a Convention of Delegates, chosen in each State by the People thereof, under the Recommendation of its Legislature, for their Assent and Ratification; and that each Convention assenting to, and ratifying the Same, should give Notice thereof to the United States in Congress assembled. Resolved, That it is the Opinion of this Convention, that as soon as the Conventions of nine States shall have ratified this Constitution, the United States in Congress assembled should fix a Day on which Electors should be appointed by the States which have ratified the same, and a Day on which the Electors should assemble to vote for the President, and the Time and Place for commencing Proceedings under this Constitution.

That after such Publication the Electors should be appointed, and the Senators and Representatives elected: That the Electors should meet on the Day fixed for the Election of the President, and should transmit their Votes certified, signed, sealed and directed, as the Constitution requires, to the Secretary of the United States in Congress assembled, that the Senators and Representatives should convene at the Time and Place assigned; that the Senators should appoint a President of the Senate, for the sole purpose of receiving, opening and counting the Votes for President; and, that after he shall be chosen, the Congress, together with the President, should, without Delay, proceed to execute this Constitution.

By the unanimous Order of the Convention
Go. WASHINGTON — Presidt.
W. JACKSON Secretary.

*Congress of the United States begun and held at the City of New-York, on Wednesday the fourth of March, one thousand seven hundred and eighty-nine

THE Conventions of a number of the States, having at the time of their adopting the Constitution, expressed a

---

* On September 25, 1789, Congress transmitted to the state legislatures twelve proposed amendments, two of which, having to do with Congressional representation and Congressional pay, were not immediately adopted. The remaining ten amendments became the Bill of Rights.

desire, in order to prevent misconstruction or abuse of its powers, that further declaratory and restrictive clauses should be added: And as extending the ground of public confidence in the Government, will best ensure the beneficent ends of its institution:

RESOLVED by the Senate and House of Representatives of the United States of America, in Congress assembled, two thirds of both Houses concurring, that the following Articles be proposed to the Legislatures of the several States, as Amendments to the Constitution of the United States, all or any of which Articles, when ratified by three fourths of the said Legislatures, to be valid to all intents and purposes, as part of the said Constitution; viz.

ARTICLES in addition to, and Amendment of the Constitution of the United States of America, proposed by Congress, and ratified by the Legislatures of the several States, pursuant to the fifth Article of the original Constitution. . . .

FREDERICK AUGUSTUS MUHLENBERG, Speaker of the House of Representatives. JOHN ADAMS, Vice-President of the United States, and President of the Senate. ATTEST, JOHN BECKLEY, Clerk of the House of Representatives. SAM. A. OTIS Secretary of the Senate.

AMENDMENTS TO THE
CONSTITUTION OF THE UNITED
STATES OF AMERICA

Amendment I*

Congress shall make no law respecting an establishment of religion, or prohibiting the free exercise thereof; or abridging the freedom of speech, or of the press; or the right of the people peaceably to assemble, and to petition the Government for a redress of grievances.

Amendment II

A well regulated Militia, being necessary to the security of a free State, the right of the people to keep and bear Arms, shall not be infringed.

Amendment III

No Soldier shall, in time of peace be quartered in any house, without the consent of the Owner, nor in time of war, but in a manner to be prescribed by law.

Amendment IV

The right of the people to be secure in their persons, houses, papers, and effects, against unreasonable searches and

---

* The first ten Amendments (Bill of Rights) were ratified effective December 15, 1791.

seizures, shall not be violated, and no Warrants shall issue, but upon probable cause, supported by Oath or affirmation, and particularly describing the place to be searched, and the persons or things to be seized.

Amendment V

No person shall be held to answer for a capital, or otherwise infamous crime, unless on a presentment or indictment of a Grand Jury, except in cases arising in the land or naval forces, or in the Militia, when in actual service in time of War or public danger; nor shall any person be subject for the same offence to be twice put in jeopardy of life or limb; nor shall be compelled in any criminal case to be a witness against himself, nor be deprived of life, liberty, or property, without due process of law; nor shall private property be taken for public use, without just compensation.

Amendment VI

In all criminal prosecutions, the accused shall enjoy the right to a speedy and public trial, by an impartial jury of the State and district wherein the crime shall have been committed; which district shall have been previously ascertained by law, and to be informed of the nature and cause of the accusation; to be confronted with the witnesses against him; to have compulsory process for obtaining witnesses in his favor, and to have the Assistance of Counsel for his defence.

Amendment VII

In Suits at common law, where the value in controversy shall exceed twenty dollars, the right of trial by jury shall be preserved, and no fact tried by a jury shall be otherwise reexamined in any Court of the United States, than according to the rules of the common law.

Amendment VIII

Excessive bail shall not be required, nor excessive fines imposed, nor cruel and unusual punishments inflicted.

Amendment IX

The enumeration in the Constitution of certain rights shall not be construed to deny or disparage others retained by the people.

Amendment X

The powers not delegated to the United States by the Constitution, nor prohibited by it to the States, are reserved to the States respectively, or to the people.

Amendment XI
[The Eleventh Amendment was ratified
February 7, 1795.]

The Judicial power of the United States shall not be the construed to extend to any suit in law or equity, commenced or prosecuted against one of the United States by Citizens of another State, or by Citizens or subjects of any Foreign State.

Amendment XII

[The Twelfth Amendment was ratified June 15, 1804.]

The Electors shall meet in their respective states and vote by ballot for President and Vice President, one of whom, at least, shall not be an inhabitant of the same state with themselves; they shall name in their ballots the person voted for as President, and in distinct ballots the person voted for as Vice-President, and they shall make distinct lists of all persons voted for as President, and of all persons voted for as Vice-President, and of the number of votes for each, which lists they shall sign and certify, and transmit sealed to the seat of the government of the United States, directed to the President of the Senate;—The President of the Senate shall, in the presence of the Senate and House of Representatives, open all the certificates and the votes shall then be counted;—The person having the greatest number of votes for President, shall be the President, if such number be a majority of the whole number of Electors appointed; and if no person have such majority, then from the persons having the highest numbers not exceeding three on the list of those voted for as President, the House of Representatives shall choose immediately, by ballot, the President. But in choosing the President, the votes shall be taken by states, the representation from each state having one vote; a quorum for this purpose shall consist of a member or members from two-thirds of the states, and a majority of all the states shall be necessary to a choice. [And if the House of Representatives shall not choose a President whenever the right of choice shall devolve upon them before the fourth day of March next following, then the Vice-President shall act as President, as in the case of the death or other constitutional disability of the President—]* The person having the greatest number of votes as Vice-President, shall be the Vice-President, if such number be a majority of the whole number of Electors appointed, and if no person have a majority, then from the two highest numbers on the list, the Senate shall choose the Vice-President; a quorum for the purpose shall consist of two-thirds of the whole number of Senators, and a majority of the whole number shall be necessary to a choice. But no person constitutionally ineligible to the office of President shall be eligible to that of Vice-President of the United States.

Amendment XIII

[The Thirteenth Amendment was ratified December 6, 1865.]

Section 1.

Neither slavery nor involuntary servitude, except as a punishment for crime whereof the party shall have been duly convicted, shall exist within the United States, or any place subject to their jurisdiction.

---

* Superseded by Section 3 of the Twentieth Amendment.

Section 2.

Congress shall have power to enforce this article by appropriate legislation.

Amendment XIV

[The Fourteenth Amendment was ratified July 9, 1868.]

Section 1.

All persons born or naturalized in the United States and subject to the jurisdiction thereof, are citizens of the United States and of the State wherein they reside. No State shall make or enforce any law which shall abridge the privileges or immunities of citizens of the United States; nor shall any State deprive any person of life, liberty, or property, without due process of law; nor deny to any person within its jurisdiction the equal protection of the laws.

Section 2.

Representatives shall be apportioned among the several States according to their respective numbers, counting the whole number of persons in each State excluding Indians not taxed. But when the right to vote at any election for the choice of electors for President and Vice President of the United States, Representatives in Congress, the Executive and Judicial officers of a State, or the members of the Legislature thereof, is denied to any of the male inhabitants of such State, being twenty-one years of age, and citizens of the United States, or in any way abridged, except for participation in rebellion, or other crime, the basis of representation therein shall be reduced in the proportion which the number of such male citizens shall bear to the whole number of male citizens twenty-one years of age in such State.

Section 3.
No person shall be a Senator or Representative in Congress, or elector of President and Vice President, or hold any office, civil or military under the United States or under any State, who having previously taken an oath, as a member of Congress, or as an officer of the United States, or as a member of any State legislature, or as an executive or judicial officer of any State, to support the Constitution of the United States, shall have engaged in Insurrection or rebellion against the same, or given aid or comfort to the enemies thereof. But Congress may by a vote of two thirds of each House, remove such disability.

Section 4.
The validity of the public debt of the United States, authorized by law, including debts incurred for payment of pensions and bounties for services in suppressing insurrection or rebellion, shall not be questioned. But neither the United States nor any State shall assume or pay any debt or obligation incurred in aid of insurrection or rebellion against the United States, or any claim for the loss or emancipation of any slave; but all such debts, obligations and claims shall be held illegal and void.

Section 5.
The Congress shall have power to enforce, by appropriate legislation, the provisions of this article.

Amendment XV

*[The Fifteenth Amendment was ratified
February 3, 1870.]*

Section 1.

The right of citizens of the United States to vote shall not be denied or abridged by the United States or by any State on account of race, color, or previous condition of servitude.

Section 2.

The Congress shall have power to enforce this article by appropriate legislation.

Amendment XVI

*[The Sixteenth Amendment was ratified
February 3, 1913.]*

The Congress shall have power to lay and collect taxes on incomes, from whatever source derived, without apportionment among the several States, and without regard to any census or enumeration.

Amendment XVII

*[The Seventeenth Amendment was ratified
April 8, 1913.]*

The Senate of the United States shall be composed of two Senators from each State, elected by the people thereof, for six years; and each Senator shall have one vote. The electors in each State shall have the qualifications requisite for electors of the most numerous branch of the State legislatures.

When vacancies happen in the representation of any State in the Senate, the executive authority of such State shall issue writs of election to fill such vacancies: *Provided,* That the legislature of any State may empower the executive thereof to make temporary appointments until the people fill the vacancies by election as the legislature may direct.

This amendment shall not be so construed as to affect the election or term of any Senator chosen before it becomes valid as part of the Constitution.

Amendment XVIII*

[The Eighteenth Amendment was ratified January 16, 1919.]

Section 1.

[After one year from the ratification of this article the manufacture, sale, or transportation of intoxicating liquors within, the importation thereof into, or the exportation thereof from the United States and all territory subject to the jurisdiction thereof for beverage purposes is hereby prohibited.

---

* The Eighteenth Amendment was repealed by the Twenty-first Amendment, December 5, 1933.

Section 2.
The Congress and the several States shall have concurrent power to enforce this article by appropriate legislation.

Section 3.
This article shall be inoperative unless it shall have been ratified as an amendment to the Constitution by the legislatures of the several States, as provided in the Constitution, within seven years from the date of the submission hereof to the States by the Congress.]

Amendment XIX
[The Nineteenth Amendment was ratified
August 18, 1920.]

The right of citizens of the United States to vote shall not be denied or abridged by the United States or by any State on account of sex.

Congress shall have power to enforce this article by appropriate legislation.

Amendment XX
[The Twentieth Amendment was ratified
January 23, 1933.]

Section 1.
The terms of the President and Vice President shall end at noon on the 20th day of January, and the terms of Senators and Representatives at noon on the 3rd day of January, of the years in which such terms would have

ended if this article had not been ratified; and the terms of their successors shall then begin.

Section 2.

The Congress shall assemble at least once in every year, and such meeting shall begin at noon on the 3rd day of January, unless they shall by law appoint a different day.

Section 3.

If, at the time fixed for the beginning of the term of the President, the President elect shall have died, the Vice President elect shall become President. If a President shall not have been chosen before the time fixed for the beginning of his term, or if the President elect shall have failed to qualify, then the Vice President elect shall act as President until a President shall have qualified; and the Congress may by law provide for the case wherein neither a President elect nor a Vice President elect shall have qualified, declaring who shall then act as President, or the manner in which one who is to act shall be selected, and such person shall act accordingly until a President or Vice President shall have qualified.

Section 4.

The Congress may by law provide for the case of the death of any of the persons from whom the House of Representatives may choose a President whenever the right of choice shall have devolved upon them, and for the case of the death of any of the persons from whom the Senate may choose a Vice President whenever the right of choice shall have devolved upon them.

Section 5.

Sections 1 and 2 shall take effect on the 15th day of October following the ratification of this article.

Section 6.

This article shall be inoperative unless it shall have been ratified as an amendment to the Constitution by the legislatures of three-fourths of the several States within seven years from the date of its submission.

Amendment XXI

[The Twenty-first Amendment was ratified December 5, 1933.]

Section 1.

The eighteenth article of amendment to the Constitution of the United States is hereby repealed.

Section 2.

The transportation or importation into any State, Territory, or possession of the United States for delivery or use therein of intoxicating liquors, in violation of the laws thereof, is hereby prohibited.

Section 3.

This article shall be inoperative unless it shall have been ratified as an amendment to the Constitution by conventions in the several States, as provided in the Constitution, within seven years from the date of the submission hereof to the States by the Congress.

Amendment XXII

*[The Twenty-second Amendment was ratified
February 27, 1951.]*

Section 1.

No person shall be elected to the office of the President more than twice, and no person who has held the office of President, or acted as President for more than two years of a term to which some other person was elected President shall be elected to the office of President more than once. But this Article shall not apply to any person holding the office of President when this Article was proposed by the Congress, and shall not prevent any person who may be holding the office of President, or acting as President, during the term within which this Article becomes operative from holding the office of President or acting as President during the remainder of such term.

Section 2.

This article shall be inoperative unless it shall have been ratified as an amendment to the Constitution by the legislatures of three-fourths of the several States within seven years from the date of its submission to the States by the Congress.

Amendment XXIII

*[The Twenty-third Amendment was ratified
March 29, 1961.]*

Section 1.

The District constituting the seat of Government of the
United States shall appoint in such manner as the
Congress may direct:

A number of electors of President and Vice President equal
to the whole number of Senators and Representatives in
Congress to which the District would be entitled if it were
a State, but in no event more than the least populous state;
they shall be in addition to those appointed by the States,
but they shall be considered, for the purposes of the election
of President and Vice President, to be electors appointed by
a state; and they shall meet in the District and perform such
duties as provided by the twelfth article of amendment.

Section 2.

The Congress shall have power to enforce this article by
appropriate legislation.

Amendment XXIV

*[The Twenty-fourth Amendment was ratified
January 23, 1964.]*

Section 1.

The right of citizens of the United States to vote in any
primary or other election for President or Vice President,
for electors for President or Vice President, or for Senator

or Representative in Congress, shall not be denied or abridged by the United States or any State by reason of failure to pay any poll tax or other tax.

Section 2.

The Congress shall have power to enforce this article by appropriate legislation.

Amendment XXV

[The Twenty-fifth Amendment was ratified February 10, 1967.]

Section 1.

In case of the removal of the President from office or of his death or resignation, the Vice President shall become President.

Section 2.

Whenever there is a vacancy in the office of the Vice President, the President shall nominate a Vice President who shall take office upon confirmation by a majority vote of both Houses of Congress.

Section 3.

Whenever the President transmits to the President pro tempore of the Senate and the Speaker of the House of Representatives his written declaration that he is unable to discharge the powers and duties of his office, and until he transmits to them a written declaration to the contrary, such powers and duties shall be discharged by the Vice President as Acting President.

Section 4.

Whenever the Vice President and a majority of either the principal officers of the executive departments or of such other body as Congress may by law provide, transmit to the President pro tempore of the Senate and the Speaker of the House of Representatives their written declaration that the President is unable to discharge the powers and duties of his office, the Vice President shall immediately assume the powers and duties of the office as Acting President.

Thereafter, when the President transmits to the President pro tempore of the Senate and the Speaker of the House of Representatives his written declaration that no inability exists, he shall resume the powers and duties of his office unless the Vice President and a majority of either the principal officers of the executive department or of such other body as Congress may by law provide, transmit within four days to the President pro tempore of the Senate and the Speaker of the House of Representatives their written declaration that the President is unable to discharge the powers and duties of his office. Thereupon Congress shall decide the issue, assembling within forty-eight hours for that purpose if not in session. If the Congress, within twenty-one days after receipt of the latter written declaration, or, if Congress is not in session, within twenty-one days after Congress is required to assemble, determines by two-thirds vote of both Houses that the President is unable to discharge the powers and duties of his office, the Vice President shall continue to discharge the same as Acting

President; otherwise, the President shall resume the powers and duties of his office.

Amendment XXVI

[The Twenty-sixth Amendment was ratified July 1, 1971.]

Section 1.

The right of citizens of the United States, who are eighteen years of age or older, to vote shall not be denied or abridged by the United States or by any State on account of age.

Section 2.

The Congress shall have power to enforce this article by appropriate legislation.

Amendment XXVII

[The Twenty-seventh Amendment was proposed on September 25, 1789, and ratified, 203 years later, on May 7, 1992.]

No law, varying the compensation for the services of the Senators and Representatives, shall take effect, until an election of Representatives shall have intervened.

THE DECLARATION OF INDEPENDENCE

ACTION OF SECOND CONTINENTAL CONGRESS, July 4, 1776.

The unanimous Declaration of the thirteen United States of America

When in the Course of human Events, it becomes necessary for one People to dissolve the Political Bands which have connected them with another, and to assume among the Powers of the Earth, the separate and equal Station to which the Laws of Nature and of Nature's God entitle them, a decent Respect to the Opinions of Mankind requires that they should declare the causes which impel them to the Separation.

We hold these truths to be self-evident, that all Men are created equal, that they are endowed by their Creator with certain unalienable Rights, that among these are Life, Liberty, and the Pursuit of Happiness—That to secure these Rights, Governments are instituted among Men, deriving their just Powers from the Consent of the Governed, that whenever any Form of Government becomes destructive of these Ends, it is the Right of the People to alter or to abolish it, and to institute new Government, laying its Foundation on such Principles, and organizing its Powers in such Form, as to them shall seem most likely to effect their Safety and Happiness. Prudence, indeed, will dictate that Governments long established should not be changed for light and transient Causes; and accordingly all Experience hath shewn, that Mankind are more disposed to suffer, while Evils are sufferable, than to right themselves by abolishing the Forms to which they are accustomed. But when a long Train of Abuses and Usurpations, pursuing invariably the same Object, evinces a Design to reduce them under absolute Despotism, it is their Right, it is their Duty, to throw off such Government, and to provide new Guards for their future Security. Such has been the patient Sufferance of these Colonies; and such is now the Necessity which constrains them to alter their former Systems of Government. The History of the present King of Great-Britain is a History of repeated Injuries and Usurpations, all having in direct Object the Establishment of an absolute Tyranny over these States. To prove this, let Facts be submitted to a candid World.

He has refused his Assent to Laws, the most wholesome and necessary for the public Good.

He has forbidden his Governors to pass Laws of immediate and pressing Importance, unless suspended in their Operation till his Assent should be obtained; and when so suspended, he has utterly neglected to attend to them.

He has refused to pass other Laws for the Accommodation of large Districts of People, unless those People would relinquish the Right of Representation in the Legislature, a Right inestimable to them, and formidable to Tyrants only.

He has called together Legislative Bodies at Places unusual, uncomfortable, and distant from the

Depository of their public Records, for the sole Purpose of fatiguing them into Compliance with his Measures.

He has dissolved Representative Houses repeatedly, for opposing with manly Firmness his Invasions on the Rights of the People.

He has refused for a long Time, after such Dissolutions, to cause others to be elected; whereby the Legislative Powers, incapable of Annihilation, have returned to the People at large for their exercise; the State remaining in the mean time exposed to all the Dangers of Invasion from without, and Convulsions within.

He has endeavoured to prevent the Population of these States; for that Purpose obstructing the Laws for Naturalization of Foreigners; refusing to pass others to encourage their Migrations hither, and raising the Conditions of new Appropriations of Lands.

He has obstructed the Administration of Justice, by refusing his Assent to Laws for establishing Judiciary Powers.

He has made Judges dependent on his Will alone, for the Tenure of their Offices, and the Amount and Payment of their Salaries.

He has erected a Multitude of new Offices, and sent hither Swarms of Officers to harrass our People, and eat out their Substance.

He has kept among us, in Times of Peace, Standing Armies, without the consent of our Legislatures.

He has affected to render the Military independent of and superior to the Civil Power.

He has combined with others to subject us to a Jurisdiction foreign to our Constitution, and unacknowledged by our Laws; giving his Assent to their Acts of pretended Legislation:

For quartering large Bodies of Armed Troops among us:

For protecting them, by a mock Trial, from Punishment for any Murders which they should commit on the Inhabitants of these States:

For cutting off our Trade with all Parts of the World:

For imposing Taxes on us without our Consent:

For depriving us, in many Cases, of the Benefits of Trial by Jury:

For transporting us beyond Seas to be tried for pretended Offences:

For abolishing the free System of English Laws in a neighbouring Province, establishing therein an arbitrary Government, and enlarging its Boundaries, so as to render it at once an Example and fit Instrument for introducing the same absolute Rule into these Colonies:

For taking away our Charters, abolishing our most valuable Laws, and altering fundamentally the Forms of our Governments:

For suspending our own Legislatures, and declaring themselves invested with Power to legislate for us in all Cases whatsoever.

He has abdicated Government here, by declaring us out of his Protection and waging War against us.

He has plundered our Seas, ravaged our Coasts, burnt our Towns, and destroyed the Lives of our People.

He is, at this Time, transporting large Armies of foreign Mercenaries to compleat the Works of Death, Desolation, and Tyranny, already begun with circumstances of Cruelty and Perfidy, scarcely paralleled in the most barbarous Ages, and totally unworthy the Head of a civilized Nation.

He has constrained our fellow Citizens taken Captive on the high Seas to bear Arms against their Country, to become the Executioners of their Friends and Brethren, or to fall themselves by their Hands.

He has excited domestic Insurrections amongst us, and has endeavoured to bring on the Inhabitants of our Frontiers, the merciless Indian Savages, whose known Rule of Warfare, is an undistinguished Destruction, of all Ages, Sexes and Conditions.

In every stage of these Oppressions we have Petitioned for Redress in the most humble Terms: Our repeated Petitions have been answered only by repeated Injury. A Prince, whose Character is thus marked by every act which may define a Tyrant, is unfit to be the Ruler of a free People.

Nor have we been wanting in Attentions to our British Brethren. We have warned them from Time to Time of attempts by their Legislature to extend an unwarrantable Jurisdiction over us. We have reminded them of the Circumstances of our Emigration and Settlement here. We have appealed to their native Justice and Magnanimity, and we have conjured them by the Ties of our common Kindred to disavow these Usurpations, which, would inevitably interrupt our Connections and Correspondence. They too have been deaf to the Voice of Justice and of Consanguinity. We must, therefore, acquiesce in the Necessity, which denounces our Separation, and hold them, as we hold the rest of Mankind, Enemies in War, in Peace, Friends.

We, therefore, the Representatives of the UNITED STATES OF AMERICA, in General Congress, Assembled, appealing to the Supreme Judge of the World for the Rectitude of our Intentions, do, in the Name, and by Authority of the good People of these Colonies, solemnly Publish and Declare, That these United Colonies are, and of Right ought to be, FREE AND INDEPENDENT STATES; that they are absolved from all Allegiance to the British Crown, and that all political Connection between them and the State of Great-Britain, is and ought to be totally dissolved; and that as FREE AND INDEPENDENT STATES, they have full Power to levy War, conclude Peace, contract Alliances, establish Commerce, and to do all other Acts and Things which INDEPENDENT STATES may of right do. And for the support of this Declaration, with a firm Reliance on the Protection of divine Providence, we mutually pledge to each other our Lives, our Fortunes, and our sacred Honor.

The 56 signatures on the Declaration appear in the positions indicated:

Georgia:
Button Gwinnett
Lyman Hall
George Walton

North Carolina:
William Hooper
Joseph Hewes
John Penn

South Carolina:
Edward Rutledge
Thomas Heyward, Jr.
Thomas Lynch, Jr.
Arthur Middleton

Massachusetts:
John Hancock

Maryland:
Samuel Chase
William Paca
Thomas Stone
Charles Carroll of Carrollton

Virginia:
George Wythe
Richard Henry Lee
Thomas Jefferson
Benjamin Harrison
Thomas Nelson, Jr.
Francis Lightfoot Lee
Carter Braxton

Pennsylvania:
Robert Morris
Benjamin Rush
Benjamin Franklin
John Morton
George Clymer
James Smith
George Taylor
James Wilson
George Ross

Delaware:
Caesar Rodney
George Read
Thomas McKean

New York:
William Floyd
Philip Livingston
Francis Lewis
Lewis Morris

New Jersey:
Richard Stockton
John Witherspoon
Francis Hopkinson
John Hart
Abraham Clark

New Hampshire:
Josiah Bartlett
William Whipple

Massachusetts:
Samuel Adams
John Adams
Robert Treat Paine
Elbridge Gerry

Rhode Island:
Stephen Hopkins
William Ellery

Connecticut:
Roger Sherman
Samuel Huntington
William Williams
Oliver Wolcott

New Hampshire:
Matthew Thornton

THE ARTICLES OF CONFEDERATION

Agreed to by Congress November 15, 1777; ratified and in force, March 1, 1781.

Preamble

To all to whom these Presents shall come, we the undersigned Delegates of the States affixed to our Names send greeting. Whereas the Delegates of the United States of America in Congress assembled did on the fifteenth day of November in the Year of our Lord One Thousand Seven Hundred and Seventy Seven, and in the Second Year of the Independence of America agree to certain Articles of Confederation and Perpetual Union Between the States of New Hampshire, Massachusetts bay Rhode Island and Providence Plantations, Connecticut, New York, New Jersey, Pennsylvania, Delaware, Maryland, Virginia, North Carolina, South Carolina and Georgia.

Article I. The Stile of this Confederacy shall be "The United States of America".

Article II. Each state retains its sovereignty, freedom, and independence, and every power, jurisdiction, and right, which is not by this Confederation expressly delegated to the United States, in Congress assembled.

Article III. The said States hereby severally enter into a firm league of friendship with each other, for their common defense, the security of their liberties, and their mutual and general welfare, binding themselves to assist each other, against all force offered to, or attacks made upon them, or any of them, on account of religion, sovereignty, trade, or any other pretense whatever.

Article IV. The better to secure and perpetuate mutual friendship and intercourse among the people of the different States in this Union, the free inhabitants of each of these States, paupers, vagabonds, and fugitives from justice excepted, shall be entitled to all privileges and immunities of free citizens in the several States; and the people of each State shall free ingress and regress to and from any other State, and shall enjoy therein all the privileges of trade and commerce, subject to the same duties, impositions, and restrictions as the inhabitants thereof respectively, provided that such restrictions shall not extend so far as to prevent the removal of property imported into any State, to any other State, of which the owner is an inhabitant; provided also that no imposition, duties or restriction shall be laid by any State, on the property of the United States, or either of them.

If any person guilty of, or charged with, treason, felony, or other high misdemeanor in any State, shall flee from justice, and be found in any of the United States, he shall, upon demand of the Governor or executive power of the State from which he fled, be delivered up and removed to the State having jurisdiction of his offense.

Full faith and credit shall be given in each of these

States to the records, acts, and judicial proceedings of the courts and magistrates of every other State.

Article V. For the most convenient management of the general interests of the United States, delegates shall be annually appointed in such manner as the legislatures of each State shall direct, to meet in Congress on the first Monday in November, in every year, with a power reserved to each State to recall its delegates, or any of them, at any time within the year, and to send others in their stead for the remainder of the year.

No State shall be represented in Congress by less than two, nor more than seven members; and no person shall be capable of being a delegate for more than three years in any term of six years; nor shall any person, being a delegate, be capable of holding any office under the United States, for which he, or another for his benefit, receives any salary, fees or emolument of any kind.

Each State shall maintain its own delegates in a meeting of the States, and while they act as members of the committee of the States.

In determining questions in the United States in Congress assembled, each State shall have one vote.

Freedom of speech and debate in Congress shall not be impeached or questioned in any court or place out of Congress, and the members of Congress shall be protected in their persons from arrests or imprisonments, during the time of their going to and from, and attendance on Congress, except for treason, felony, or breach of the peace.

Article VI. No State, without the consent of the United States in Congress assembled, shall send any embassy to, or receive any embassy from, or enter into any conference, agreement, alliance or treaty with any King, Prince or State; nor shall any person holding any office of profit or trust under the United States, or any of them, accept any present, emolument, office or title of any kind whatever from any King, Prince or foreign State; nor shall the United States in Congress assembled, or any of them, grant any title of nobility.

No two or more States shall enter into any treaty, confederation or alliance whatever between them, without the consent of the United States in Congress assembled, specifying accurately the purposes for which the same is to be entered into, and how long it shall continue.

No State shall lay any imposts or duties, which may interfere with any stipulations in treaties, entered into by the United States in Congress assembled, with any King, Prince or State, in pursuance of any treaties already proposed by Congress, to the courts of France and Spain.

No vessel of war shall be kept up in time of peace by any State, except such number only, as shall be deemed necessary by the United States in Congress assembled, for the defense of such State, or its trade; nor shall any body of forces be kept up by any State in time of peace, except such number only, as in the judgement of the United States in Congress assembled, shall be deemed requisite to garrison the forts necessary for the defense of such State; but every State shall always keep up a well-regulated and disciplined militia, sufficiently armed and accoutered, and shall provide and constantly have ready for use, in public stores, a due number of filed pieces and tents, and a proper quantity of arms, ammunition and camp equipage.

No State shall engage in any war without the consent of the United States in Congress assembled, unless such State be actually invaded by enemies, or shall have received certain advice of a resolution being formed by some nation of Indians to invade such State, and the danger is so imminent as not to admit of a delay till the United States in Congress assembled can be consulted; nor shall any State grant commissions to any ships or vessels of war, nor letters of marque or reprisal, except it be after a declaration of war by the United States in Congress assembled, and then only against the Kingdom or State and the subjects thereof, against which war has been so declared, and under such regulations as shall be established by the United States in Congress assembled, unless such State be infested by pirates, in which case vessels of war may be fitted out for that occasion, and kept so long as the danger shall continue, or until the United States in Congress assembled shall determine otherwise.

Article VII. When land forces are raised by any State for the common defense, all officers of or under the rank of colonel, shall be appointed by the legislature of each State respectively, by whom such forces shall be raised, or in such manner as such State shall direct, and all vacancies shall be filled up by the State which first made the appointment.

Article VIII. All charges of war, and all other expenses that shall be incurred for the common defense or general welfare, and allowed by the United States in Congress assembled, shall be defrayed out of a common treasury, which shall be supplied by the several States in proportion to the value of all land within each State, granted or surveyed for any person, as such land and the buildings and improvements thereon shall be estimated according to such mode as the United States in Congress assembled, shall from time to time direct and appoint.

The taxes for paying that proportion shall be laid and levied by the authority and direction of the legislatures of the several States within the time agreed upon by the United States in Congress assembled.

Article IX. The United States in Congress assembled, shall have the sole and exclusive right and power of determining on peace and war, except in the cases mentioned in the sixth article—of sending and receiving ambassadors—entering into treaties and alliances, provided that no treaty of commerce shall be made whereby the legislative power of the respective States shall be restrained from imposing such imposts and duties on foreigners, as their own people are subjected to, or from prohibiting the exportation or importation of any species of goods or commodities whatsoever—of establishing rules for deciding in all cases, what captures on land or water shall be legal, and in what manner prizes taken by land or naval forces in the service of the United States shall be divided or appropriated—of granting letters of marque and reprisal in times of peace—appointing courts for the trial of piracies and felonies committed on the high seas and establishing courts for receiving and determining finally appeals in all cases of captures, provided that no member of Congress shall be appointed a judge of any of the said courts.

The United States in Congress assembled shall also be the last resort on appeal in all disputes and differences now subsisting or that hereafter may arise between two or more States concerning boundary, jurisdiction or any other causes whatever; which authority shall always be exercised in the manner following. Whenever the legislative or executive authority or lawful agent of any State in controversy with another shall present a petition to Congress stating the matter in question and praying for a hearing, notice thereof shall be given by order of Congress to the legislative or executive authority of the other State in controversy, and a day assigned for the appearance of the parties by their lawful agents, who shall then be directed to appoint by joint consent, commissioners or judges to constitute a court for hearing and determining the matter in question: but if they cannot agree, Congress shall name three persons out of each of the United States, and from the list of such persons each party shall alternately strike out one, the petitioners beginning, until the number shall be reduced to thirteen; and from that number not less than seven, nor more than nine names as Congress shall direct, shall in the presence of Congress be drawn out by lot, and the persons whose names shall be so drawn or any five of them, shall be commissioners or judges, to hear and finally determine the controversy, so always as a major part of the judges who shall hear the cause shall agree in the determination: and if either party shall neglect to attend at the day appointed, without showing reasons, which Congress shall judge sufficient, or being present shall refuse to strike, the Congress shall proceed to nominate three persons out of each State, and the secretary of Congress shall strike in behalf of such party absent or refusing; and the judgement and sentence of the court to be appointed, in the manner before prescribed, shall be final and conclusive; and if any of the parties shall refuse to submit to the authority of such court, or to appear or defend their claim or cause, the court shall nevertheless proceed to pronounce sentence, or judgement, which shall in like manner be final and decisive, the judgement or sentence and other proceedings being in either case transmitted to Congress, and lodged among the acts of Congress for the security of the parties concerned: provided that every commissioner, before he sits in judgement, shall take an oath to be administered by one of the judges of the supreme or superior court of the State, where the cause shall be tried, 'well and truly to hear and determine the matter in question, according to the best of his judgement, without favor, affection or hope of reward': provided also, that no State shall be deprived of territory for the benefit of the United States.

All controversies concerning the private right of soil claimed under different grants of two or more States, whose jurisdictions as they may respect such lands, and the States which passed such grants are adjusted, the said grants or either of them being at the same time claimed to have originated antecedent to such settlement of jurisdiction, shall on the petition of either party to the Congress of the United States, be finally determined as near as may be in the same manner as is before prescribed for deciding disputes respecting territorial jurisdiction between different States.

The United States in Congress assembled shall also have the sole and exclusive right and power of regulating the alloy and value of coin struck by their own authority, or by that of the respective States—fixing the standards of weights and measures throughout the United States—regulating the trade and managing all affairs with the Indians, not members of any of the States, provided that the legislative right of any State within its own limits be not infringed or violated—establishing or regulating post offices from one State to another, throughout all the United States, and exacting such postage on the papers passing through the same as may be requisite to defray the expenses of the said office—appointing all officers of the land forces, in the service of the United States, excepting regimental officers—appointing all the officers of the naval forces, and commissioning all officers whatever in the service of the United States—making rules for the government and regulation of the said land and naval forces, and directing their operations.

The United States in Congress assembled shall have authority to appoint a committee, to sit in the recess of Congress, to be denominated 'A Committee of the States', and to consist of one delegate from each State; and to appoint such other committees and civil officers as may be necessary for managing the general affairs of the United States under their direction—to appoint one of their members to preside, provided that no person be allowed to serve in the office of president more than one year in any term of three years; to ascertain the necessary sums of money to be raised for the service of the United States, and to appropriate and apply the same for defraying the public expenses—to borrow money, or emit bills on the credit of the United States, transmitting every half-year to the respective States an account of the sums of money so borrowed or emitted—to build and equip a navy—to agree upon the number of land forces, and to make requisitions from each State for its quota, in proportion to the number of white inhabitants in such State; which requisition shall be binding, and thereupon the legislature of each State shall appoint the regimental officers, raise the men and cloath, arm and equip them in a solid-like manner, at the expense of the United States; and the officers and men so cloathed, armed and equipped shall march to the place appointed, and within the time agreed on by the United States in Congress assembled. But if the United States in Congress assembled shall, on consideration of circumstances judge proper that any State should not raise men, or should raise a smaller number of men than the quota thereof, such extra number shall be raised, officered, cloathed, armed and equipped in the same manner as the quota of each State, unless the legislature of such State shall judge that such extra number cannot be safely spread out in the same, in which case they shall raise, officer, cloath, arm and equip as many of such extra number as they judge can be safely spared. And the officers and men so cloathed, armed, and equipped, shall march to the place appointed, and within the time agreed on by the United States in Congress assembled.

The United States in Congress assembled shall never engage in a war, nor grant letters of marque or reprisal in time of peace, nor enter into any treaties or alliances, nor coin money, nor regulate the value thereof, nor ascertain the sums and expenses necessary for the defense and welfare of the United States, or any of them, nor emit bills, nor borrow money on the credit of the United States, nor appropriate money, nor agree upon the number of vessels of war, to be built or purchased, or the number of land or sea forces to be raised, nor appoint a commander in chief of the army or navy, unless nine States assent to the same: nor shall a question on any other point, except for adjourning from day to day be determined, unless by the votes of the majority of the United States in Congress assembled.

The Congress of the United States shall have power to adjourn to any time within the year, and to any place within the United States, so that no period of adjournment be for a longer duration than the space of six months, and shall publish the journal of their proceedings monthly, except such parts thereof relating to treaties, alliances or military operations, as in their judgement require secrecy; and the yeas and nays of the delegates of each State on any question shall be entered on the journal, when it is desired by any delegates of a State, or any of them, at his or their request shall be furnished with a transcript of the said journal, except such parts as are above excepted, to lay before the legislatures of the several States.

Article X. The Committee of the States, or any nine of them, shall be authorized to execute, in the recess of Congress, such of the powers of Congress as the United States in Congress assembled, by the consent of the nine States, shall from time to time think expedient to vest them with; provided that no power be delegated to the said Committee, for the exercise of which, by the Articles of Confederation, the voice of nine States in the Congress of the United States assembled be requisite.

Article XI. Canada acceding to this confederation, and adjoining in the measures of the United States, shall be admitted into, and entitled to all the advantages of this Union; but no other colony shall be admitted into the same, unless such admission be agreed to by nine States.

Article XII. All bills of credit emitted, monies borrowed, and debts contracted by, or under the authority of Congress, before the assembling of the United States, in pursuance of the present confederation, shall be deemed and considered as a charge against the United States, for payment and satisfaction whereof the said United States, and the public faith are hereby solemnly pledged.

Article XIII. Every State shall abide by the determination of the United States in Congress assembled, on all questions which by this confederation are submitted to them. And the Articles of this Confederation shall be inviolably observed by every State, and the Union shall be perpetual; nor shall any alteration at any time hereafter be made in any of them; unless such alteration be agreed to in a Congress of the United States, and be afterwards confirmed by the legislatures of every State.

And Whereas it hath pleased the Great Governor of the World to incline the hearts of the legislatures we respectively represent in Congress, to approve of, and to authorize us to ratify the said Articles of Confederation and perpetual Union. Know Ye that we the undersigned delegates, by virtue of the power and authority to us given for that purpose, do by these presents, in the name and in behalf of our respective constituents, fully and entirely ratify and confirm each and every of the said Articles of Confederation and perpetual Union, and all and singular the matters and things therein contained: And we do further solemnly plight and engage the faith of our respective constituents, that they shall abide by the determinations of the United States in Congress assembled, on all questions, which by the said Confederation are submitted to them. And that the Articles thereof shall be inviolably observed by the States we respectively represent, and that the Union shall be perpetual.

In Witness whereof we have hereunto set our hands in Congress. Done at Philadelphia in the State of Pennsylvania the ninth day of July in the Year of our Lord One Thousand Seven Hundred and Seventy-Eight, and in the Third Year of the independence of America.

On the part and behalf of the State of New Hampshire:
Josiah Bartlett
John Wentworth Junr.
August 8th 1778

On the part and behalf of The State of Massachusetts Bay: John Hancock
Francis Dana
Samuel Adams
James Lovell
Elbridge Gerry
Samuel Holten

On the part and behalf of the State of Rhode Island
and Providence Plantations:
William Ellery
John Collins
Henry Marchant

On the part and behalf of the State of Connecticut:
Roger Sherman
Titus Hosmer
Samuel Huntington
Andrew Adams
Oliver Wolcott

On the Part and Behalf of the State of New York:
James Duane
Wm Duer
Francis Lewis
Gouv Morris

On the Part and in Behalf of the State of New Jersey,
November 26, 1778:
Jno Witherspoon
Nathaniel Scudder

On the part and behalf of the State of Pennsylvania:
Robt Morris
William Clingan
Daniel Roberdeau
Joseph Reed
John Bayard Smith
22nd July 1778

On the part and behalf of the State of Delaware:
Tho Mckean February 12, 1779
John Dickinson May 5th 1779
Nicholas Van Dyke

On the part and behalf of the State of Maryland:
John Hanson March 1 1781
Daniel Carroll Do

On the Part and Behalf of the State of Virginia:
Richard Henry Lee
Jno Harvie
John Banister
Francis Lightfoot Lee
Thomas Adams

On the part and Behalf of the State of No Carolina:
John Penn July 21St 1778
Corns Harnett
Jno Williams

On the part and behalf of the State of South Carolina:
Henry Laurens
Richd Hutson
William Henry Drayton
Thos Heyward Junr
Jno Mathews

On the part and behalf of the State of Georgia:
Jno Walton 24th July 1778
Edwd Telfair
Edwd Langworthy

INDEX
to the Constitution and Amendments